Dear Ashley
Happy Birthday! 2020
You know how to make
everyone Smile!
We Love You ♡
Sally & Bernie

DAY 364

Motherhood is neither a duty nor a privilege, but simply the way that humanity can satisfy the desire for physical immortality and triumph over the fear of death.

—*Rebecca West, English author, journalist, and literary critic*

WISDOM

We are what our thoughts have made us; so take care about what you think. Words are secondary. Thoughts live; they travel far.

—*Swami Vivekananda, Indian Hindu monk*

Daily
Motherhood
365 Days
OF INSPIRATION FOR THE HARDEST
JOB YOU'LL EVER LOVE

FAMILIUS

She taught me what's important, and what isn't. And I've never forgotten. And that's what mothers do, I say.

—*Steven Herrick, Australian poet and author,* A Place Like This

WISDOM

DAY 2

No language can express the power, and beauty, and heroism, and majesty of a mother's love. It shrinks not where man cowers, and grows stronger where man faints, and over wastes of worldly fortunes sends the radiance of its quenchless fidelity like a star.

—*Edwin Hubbell Chapin,*
American preacher and editor

LOVE

HAPPINESS

Being a mom has made me so tired—and so happy.

—*Tina Fey, American actress, comedian, and author*

I want to be able to say that I lived my days consciously, knowing that I placed motherhood at the forefront, but that I also followed my passions, used my talents, and did my best to make choices that allowed me to live with clarity, purpose, and a sense of calmness to days. I want to give a deep yes to the things that really matter.

—*Sarah Turner, American writer,*
Deliberate Motherhood

STEWARDSHIP

Being a mother is learning about strengths you didn't know you had, and dealing with fears you didn't know existed.

—*Linda Wooten, American artist and poet*

STRENGTH

DAY 6

There are times as a parent when
you realize that your job is not to
be the parent you always imagined
you'd be, the parent you always
wished you had. Your job is to be
the parent your child needs, given
the particulars of his or her own life
and nature.

—*Ayelet Waldman, Israeli-American author*

RELATIONSHIPS

DAY 7

People often say that "beauty is in the eye of the beholder," and I say that the most liberating thing about beauty is realizing that *you* are the beholder. This empowers us to find beauty in places where others have not dared to look, including inside ourselves.

—*Salma Hayek, Mexican-American actress, director, and producer*

I am sure that if the mothers of various nations could meet, there would be no more wars.

—*E. M. Forster, English novelist and writer*

We need four hugs a day for survival. We need eight hugs a day for maintenance. We need twelve hugs a day for growth.

—*Virginia Satir, American author and social worker*

LOVE

I see myself as a mom first. I'm so lucky to have that role in life. The world can like me, hate me, or fall apart around me, and at least I wake up with my kids and I'm happy.

—*Angelina Jolie, American actress, filmmaker, and humanitarian*

HAPPINESS

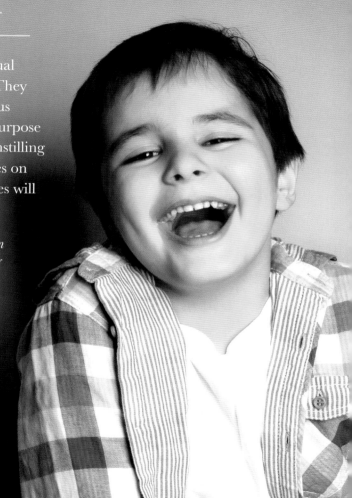

STEWARDSHIP

Children are not casual guests in our home. They have been loaned to us temporarily for the purpose of loving them and instilling a foundation of values on which their future lives will be built.

—*James Dobson, American evangelical Christian author*

STRENGTH

DAY 12

It takes someone really brave to be a mother, someone strong to raise a child, and someone special to love someone more than herself.

—*Ritu Ghatourey, Indian-American author*

DAY 13

The natural state of motherhood is unselfishness. When you
become a mother, you are no
longer the center of your own
universe. You relinquish that
position to your children.

—*Jessica Lange, American actress*

Babies are bits of stardust
blown from the hand of God.
Lucky is the woman who knows
the pangs of birth, for she has
held a star.

—*Larry Barretto, American writer*

WISDOM

My mother once told me, "When you have to make a decision, imagine the person you want to become someday. Ask yourself, what would that person do?"

—*Barry Deutsch, American cartoonist and graphic novelist,* How Mirka Met a Meteorite

At its core, mothering is motivated by love. By recognizing love as the explicit motivator behind what we do, everyday, mundane tasks suddenly become meaningful.

—*Saydi Shumway, American writer,* Deliberate Motherhood

LOVE

DAY 17

A mother's happiness is like a beacon, lighting up the future but reflected also on the past in the guise of fond memories.

—*Honoré de Balzac, French novelist and playwright*

DAY 18

Rest easy, real mothers. The very fact that you worry about being a good mom means that you already are one.

—*Jodi Picoult, American author,* House Rules

DAY 19

A strong woman understands that the gifts such as logic, decisiveness, and strength are just as feminine as intuition and emotional connection. She values and uses all of her gifts.

—*Nancy Rathburn, American author*

DAY 20

Yes, Mother. I can see you are flawed. You have not hidden it. That is your greatest gift to me.

—*Alice Walker, American author*

Even in the most beautiful music there are some silences, which are there so we can witness the importance of silence.

—*Andrea Bocelli, Italian classical tenor*

BEAUTY

DAY 22

A mother understands
what a child does not say.

—Yiddish proverb

DAY 23

Making the decision to have
a child—it's momentous.
It is to decide forever to
have your heart go walking
around outside your body.

—*Elizabeth Stone, American author*

Sometimes the laughter in mothering is the recognition in the ironies and absurdities. Sometimes, though, it's just the pure, unthinking delight.

—*Barbara Schapiro, American author and professor*

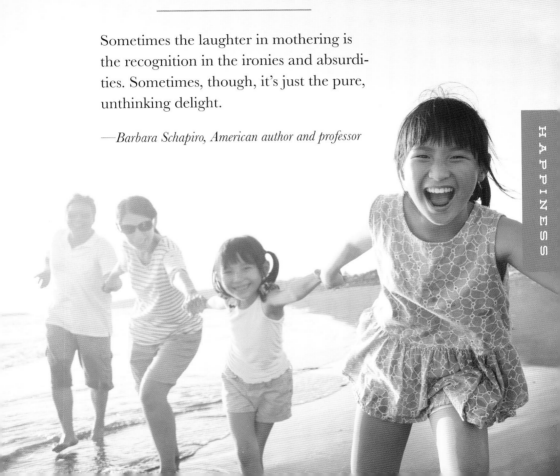

HAPPINESS

DAY 25

Mothers were meant to love us
unconditionally, to understand
our moments of stupidity, to rep-
rimand us for lame excuses while
yet acknowledging our point of
view, to weep over our pain and
failures as well as cry at our joy
and successes, and to cheer us
on despite countless start-overs.
Heaven knows, no one else will.

—*Richelle E. Goodrich, American author*

As it stands, motherhood is a sort of wilderness through which each woman hacks her way, part martyr, part pioneer; a turn of events from which some women derive feelings of heroism, while others experience a sense of exile from the world they knew.

—*Rachel Cusk, UK-based Canadian novelist and writer*

STRENGTH

Pride is one of the seven deadly sins; but it cannot be the pride of a mother in her children, for that is a compound of two cardinal virtues—faith and hope.

—*Charles Dickens, English writer and social critic,* Nicholas Nickleby

DAY 28

The best and most beautiful
things in the world cannot be seen
or even touched; they must be felt
with the heart.

—*Helen Keller, American author, political
activist, and lecturer*

BEAUTY

I am a woman in process. I'm just trying like everybody else. I try to take every conflict, every experience, and learn from it. Life is never dull.

—*Oprah Winfrey, American talk show host and philanthropist*

WISDOM

DAY 30

When you look at each load as a little gift of love to your family, laundry isn't as dull as we once thought it was.

—*Darlene Schacht, American author*

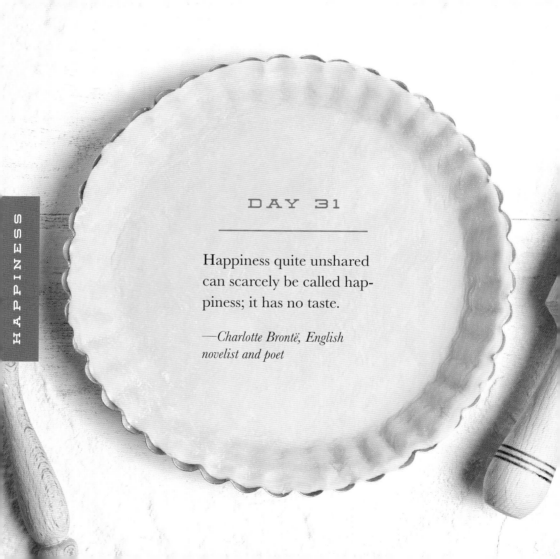

DAY 31

Happiness quite unshared can scarcely be called happiness; it has no taste.

—*Charlotte Brontë, English novelist and poet*

As we focus on nurturing our children and helping them become the people they need to be, we can and should focus on nurturing the various "powers" that reside within *us*. Personal development does not need to happen at the expense of our children's development. In fact, our children's development *depends* upon our personal development. The refiner's fire of motherhood changes you. It can make you better. We can truly become the people we really want to be through striving to become the mother we really want to be.

—*Linda Eyre, American author,* Deliberate Motherhood

STEWARDSHIP

DAY 33

A woman is like a teabag—you never know how strong she is until she gets in hot water.

Eleanor Roosevelt, former First Lady of the United States, activist, and diplomat

DAY 34

A child's hand in yours—
what tenderness and power
it arouses. You are instantly
the very touchstone of wisdom and strength.

—*Marjorie Holmes, American*
columnist and author

Mom could make small things seem miraculous. That was her talent.

— Matthew Quick, American writer

BEAUTY

Mama exhorted her children at every opportunity to "jump at de sun." We may not land on the sun, but at least we would get off the ground.

—*Zora Neale Hurston, American folklorist, anthropologist, and author,* A Biography of the Spirit

WISDOM

DAY 37

My mother's love has always been a sustaining force for our family, and one of my greatest joys is seeing her integrity, her compassion, her intelligence reflected in my daughters.

—*Michelle Obama, American First Lady*

The joy in motherhood comes in moments. There will be hard times and frustrating times, but amid the challenges, there are shining moments of joy and satisfaction.

—*M. Russell Ballard, American author and religious leader*

HAPPINESS

DAY 39

Mother is a verb, not a noun.

—*Anonymous*

Do not pray for an easy life;
pray for the strength to endure a
difficult one.

—*Bruce Lee, Hong Kong-American
martial artist and actor*

STRENGTH

Listen earnestly to anything your children want to tell you, no matter what. If you don't listen to the little stuff when they're little, they won't tell you the big stuff when they're big. Because to them, all of it has always been big stuff.

—*Catherine M. Wallace,*
American author

Strength of character may be learned at work, but beauty of character is learned at home.

—*Henry Drummond, Scottish evangelist, writer, and lecturer*

BEAUTY

DAY 43

Don't judge each day by the harvest you reap, but by the seeds that you plant.

—*Robert Louis Stevenson, Scottish novelist, poet, essayist, and travel writer*

Love as powerful as your mother's for you leaves its own mark. To have been loved so deeply, even though the person who loved us is gone, will give us some protection forever.

—*J. K. Rowling, English novelist,* Harry Potter and the Sorcerer's Stone

LOVE

In our desires to find solutions to life's real problems, we too often turn to an attack on motherhood. Mothering children, in many circles, is being defined as madness. It's described as mind-numbing, menial work akin to prison or slavery. Mothers are portrayed as not having time to change the world because they're "wasting" their time in their homes. Children are labeled as detriments to a woman's personal growth, and the decision to become a mother is reduced to its impact on paychecks, freedom, and personal satisfaction. Motherhood, then, becomes a decision based solely on logic.

What many women don't understand . . . is this one true principle: motherhood defies logic. . . . For those of us (mothers or not) who know the power of motherhood, it is our privilege to cherish it and to defend it. . . . And I'm doing everything in my power to teach [my children] what my mom knew all along: that motherhood, as illogical as it may be, is absolutely worth it.

—*April Perry, co-founder of Power of Moms,* Motherhood Realized

DAY 46

There are only two lasting
bequests we can hope to give
our children. One of these is
roots; the other, wings.

—*Hodding Carter, American
journalist and author*

DAY 47

Courage is like a muscle. We strengthen it by use.

—*Ruth Gordon, American actress*

A mother is not a person to lean on but a person to make leaning unnecessary.

—*Dorothy Canfield Fisher, American educational reformer, social activist, and author*

DAY 49

The most beautiful people we have known are those who have known defeat, known suffering, known struggle, known loss, and have found their way out of the depths. Beautiful people do not just happen.

—*Elisabeth Kübler-Ross, Swiss-born psychiatrist and author*

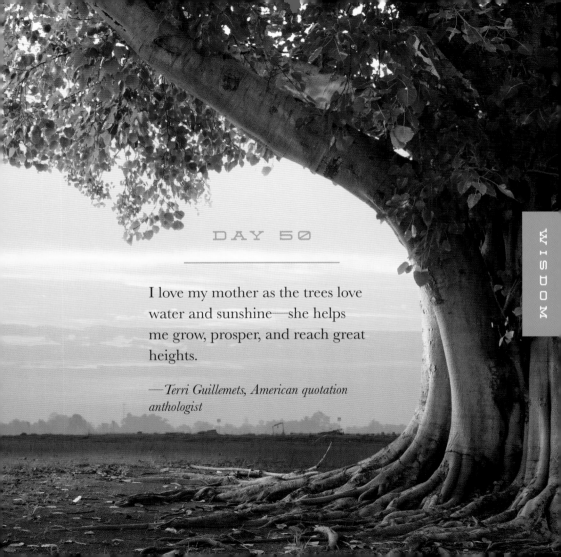

DAY 50

I love my mother as the trees love water and sunshine—she helps me grow, prosper, and reach great heights.

—*Terri Guillemets, American quotation anthologist*

WISDOM

If you want others to be happy, practice compassion. If you want to be happy, practice compassion.

—*Dalai Lama, Tibetan Buddhist spiritual leader*

LOVE

The most wasted of all days
is one without laughter.

—*Nicolas Chamfort, French author*

HAPPINESS

STEWARDSHIP

DAY 53

You will come to know that
what appears today to be a
sacrifice will prove instead to
be the greatest investment that
you will ever make.

—*Gordon B. Hinckley, American
author and religious leader*

Successful mothers are not the ones that have never struggled. They are the ones that never give up, despite the struggles.

—*Sharon Jaynes, American author*

STRENGTH

DAY 55

The art of mothering is to teach the art of living to children.

—Elaine Heffner, psychotherapist and parent educator

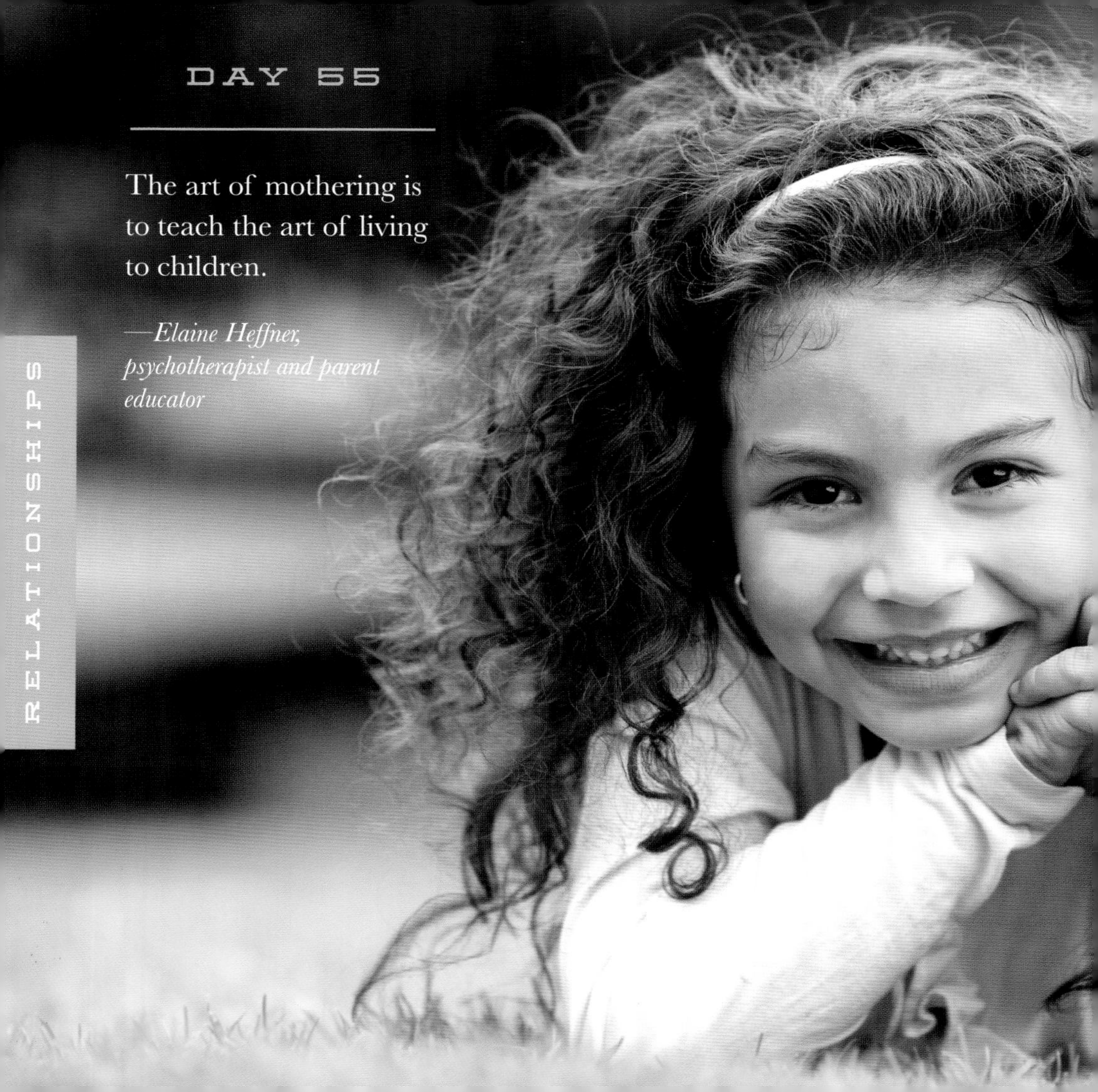

The beauty of a woman is not in the clothes she wears, the figure that she carries, or the way she combs her hair. The beauty of a woman is seen in her eyes, because that is the doorway to her heart, the place where love resides. True beauty in a woman is reflected in her soul. It's the caring that she lovingly gives, the passion that she shows, and the beauty of a woman only grows with passing years.

—Audrey Hepburn, English actress and humanitarian

BEAUTY

DAY 57

Counsel woven into the fabric
of real life is wisdom.

—*Walter Benjamin, German literary*
critic and philosopher

DAY 58

A good mother loves fiercely
but ultimately brings up her
children to thrive without her.

—*Erin Kelly, British novelist,* The
Burning Air

DAY 59

I once came across a sign that said, "While in the pursuit of happiness, one should stop and just be happy." For me this sums it up. Because the truth is, moments are fleeting and minutes soon turn into memories. I want the sweet moments of motherhood to be breathed in, savored, and always remembered.

—*Emily Ashton, American writer,* Motherhood Realized

DAY 60

My mother gave me life and never asked for anything in return. That is her secret you know, always giving without any expectations. She is as constant as the sunrise, the moon, the stars, and I count on her. She helps me find my way through the years and makes me laugh while doing it.

—*Unknown*

STEWARDSHIP

DAY 61

We gain strength, and courage, and confidence by each experience in which we really stop to look fear in the face . . . we must do that which we think we cannot.

—Eleanor Roosevelt, former First Lady of the United States, activist, and diplomat

DAY 62

Mother is the name for God
in the lips and hearts of
little children.

—*William Makepeace Thackeray,*
English novelist

There is nothing more beautiful than someone who goes out of their way to make life beautiful for others.

—*Mandy Hale, American author and speaker*

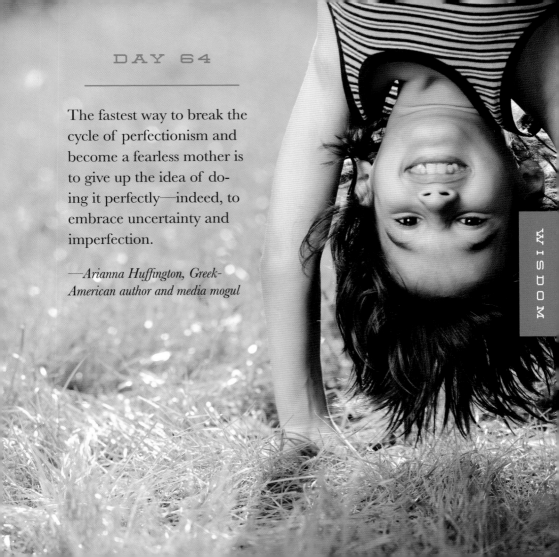

The fastest way to break the cycle of perfectionism and become a fearless mother is to give up the idea of doing it perfectly—indeed, to embrace uncertainty and imperfection.

—*Arianna Huffington, Greek-American author and media mogul*

WISDOM

Mother's love is bliss, is peace, it need not be acquired, it need not be deserved. If it is there, it is like a blessing; if it is not there, it is as if all the beauty had gone out of life.

—*Erich Fromm, German psychologist*

LOVE

DAY 66

Be happy for this moment. This moment is your life.

—*Omar Khayyam, Persian mathematician, astronomer, philosopher, and poet*

DAY 67

There will be so many times
you feel like you've failed,
but in the eyes, heart, and
mind of your child, you are
Supermom.

—*Stephanie Precourt, American
writer and blogger*

DAY 68

Don't be pushed by your problems. Be led by your dreams.

—Ralph Waldo Emerson, American essayist, lecturer, and poet

DAY 69

The moment a child is born,
the mother is also born.
She never existed before.
The woman existed, but the
mother, never. A mother is
something absolutely new.

—*Rajneesh, Indian mystic, guru, and
spiritual teacher*

You never understand life until it grows inside of you.

—Sandra Chami Kassis, Lebanese author

BEAUTY

Motherhood has a very humanizing effect. Everything gets reduced to essentials.

—*Meryl Streep, American actress*

WISDOM

Motherhood: All love
begins and ends there.

—*Robert Browning, English
poet and playwright*

LOVE

DAY 73

I, not events, have the power to make me happy or unhappy today. I can choose which it shall be. Yesterday is dead, tomorrow hasn't arrived yet. I have just one day, today, and I'm going to be happy in it.

—*Groucho Marx, American comedian and actor*

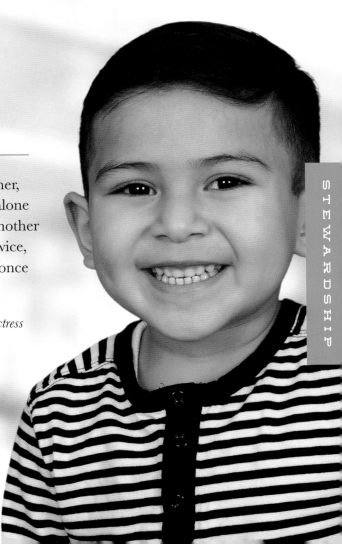

DAY 74

When you are a mother,
you are never really alone
in your thoughts. A mother
always has to think twice,
once for herself and once
for her child.

—*Sophia Loren, Italian actress*

STEWARDSHIP

Nobody can go back and start a
new beginning, but anyone can start
today and make a new ending.

—*Maria Robinson, author*

STRENGTH

You are exactly who your children need. No one can fill your shoes. No one can give what you have to offer. No one can love or know your child like you do. That is the privilege of being a mother.

—*Catherine Arveseth, American writer,* Motherhood Realized

DAY 77

No painter's brush, nor poet's pen

In justice to her fame

Has ever reached half high enough

To write a mother's name.

—*Unknown*

I believe the choice to become a mother is the choice to become one of the greatest spiritual teachers there is.

—*Oprah Winfrey, American talk show host and philanthropist*

WISDOM

LOVE

DAY

A loving heart is the beginning
of all knowledge.

—*Thomas Carlyle, Scottish philosopher,
satirical writer, and teacher*

DAY 80

A mother is a woman who shows you the light when you just see the dark.

—*Robin Grimaldos, French author and academic*

DAY 81

The work of a mother is hard,
too often unheralded work.
Please know that it is worth it
then, now, and forever.

—*Jeffrey R. Holland, American
educator and religious leader*

My mother taught me about the power of inspiration and courage, and she did it with a strength and a passion that I wish could be bottled.

—*Carly Fiorina, American businesswoman, author, and politician*

STRENGTH

When I stopped seeing my mother with the eyes of a child, I saw the woman who helped me give birth to myself.

—*Nancy Friday, American author*

RELATIONSHIPS

As my mom always said,
"You'd rather have smile lines
than frown lines."

— *Cindy Crawford, American model*

BEAUTY

We are made wise not
by the recollection of
our past, but by the
responsibility for our
future.

—*George Bernard Shaw,*
Irish playwright

WISDOM

A mother's love for her child is like nothing else in the world. It knows no law, no pity, it dares all things and crushes down remorselessly all that stands in its path.

—*Agatha Christie, English novelist,*
"The Last Séance"

LOVE

In the end, I am the only one who can give my children a happy mother who loves life.

—*Janene Wolsey Baadsgaard,
American author and writer*

HAPPINESS

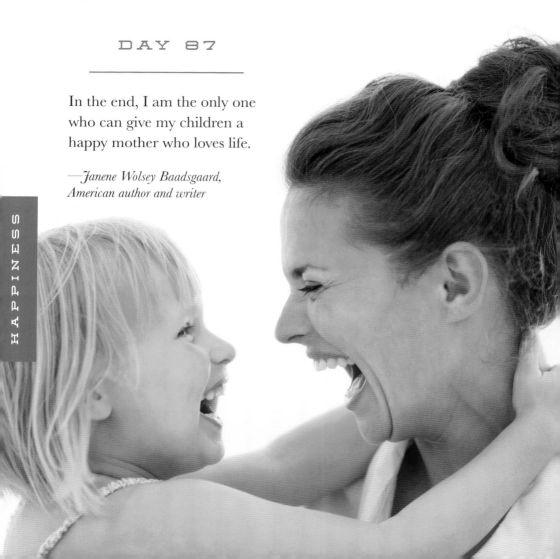

How beautifully everything is arranged by Nature; as soon as a child enters the world, it finds a mother ready to take care of it.

—*Jules Michelet, French historian*

STEWARDSHIP

Nothing that doesn't push
you past your limits can
change your life. It's true of
work, it's true of parenting,
and it's true—a hundred
times over—of love.

—*Katherine Center, American
author,* Nothing Worthwhile
Is Ever Easy

STRENGTH

DAY 90

A child is your legacy.
What better thing you can
do in life than put a really
good person in the world
who's going to make it a
better place?

— Alexis Stewart, American
television host and radio personality

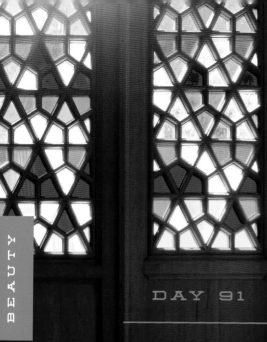

DAY 91

People are like stained-glass windows.
They sparkle and shine when the sun is
out, but when the darkness sets in, their
true beauty is revealed only if there is a
light from within.

—*Elisabeth Kübler-Ross, Swiss-born psychiatrist and
author*

The only true wisdom is in
knowing you know nothing.

—*Socrates, classical Greek philosopher*

WISDOM

DAY 93

Love can solve a multitude of problems. It can cover up our mistakes. It can make us resilient. It is the strongest antidote to our most serious dilemmas as mothers. While it won't always magically fix or change everything, it will fix and change us.

—*Saydi Shumway, American writer,* Deliberate Motherhood

My mother told me,
"The best weapon in
life is the smile."

—*Simon Porte Jacquemus,*
French fashion designer

HAPPINESS

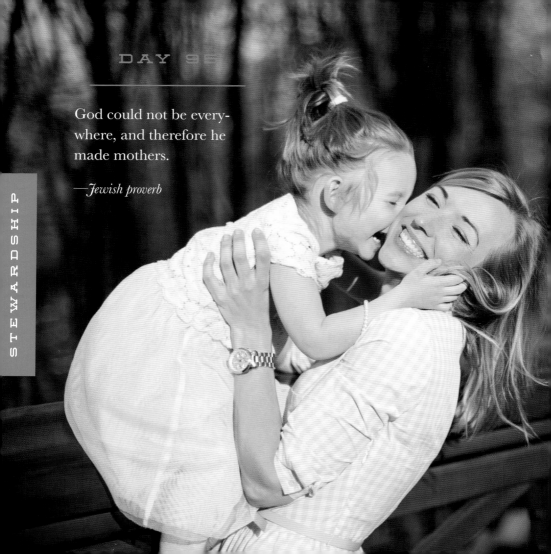

God could not be every-
where, and therefore he
made mothers.

—*Jewish proverb*

STEWARDSHIP

DAY 96

A hero is an ordinary individual
who finds the strength to persevere
and endure in spite of overwhelming obstacles.

—*Christopher Reeve, American actor*

RELATIONSHIPS

The bond between mothers and their children is one defined by love. As a mother's prayers for her children are unending, so are the wisdom, grace, and strength they provide to their children.

—*George W. Bush, former president of the United States*

DAY 98

For beautiful eyes, look for the good in others; for beautiful lips, speak only words of kindness; and for poise, walk with the knowledge that you are never alone.

—*Audrey Hepburn, English actress and humanitarian*

DAY 99

It is not until you become a mother that your judgment slowly turns to compassion and understanding.

—*Erma Bombeck, American humorist and author*

DAY 100

The heart of a mother is a
deep abyss at the bottom of
which you will always find
forgiveness.

*— Honoré de Balzac, French novelist
and playwright*

DAY 101

Happiness is not a goal; it's a
by-product of a life well lived.

—*Eleanor Roosevelt, former First
Lady of the United States, activist, and
diplomat*

DAY 102

Only mothers can think of the future—because they give birth to it in their children.

—*Maxim Gorky, Russian writer and political activist*

DAY 108

Challenges are what make life interesting
and overcoming them is what makes life
meaningful.

—*Joshua J. Marine, American author*

DAY 106

It's not what you look at that matters; it's what you see.

—*Henry David Thoreau, American author, poet, and philosopher*

Mothers observe all, absorb all, give all, forgive all, offer all, suffer all, feel all, heal all, hope for all, pray for all. But most of all, Mothers *love* always.

—*Richelle E. Goodrich, American author*

LOVE

Happiness is holding someone in your arms and knowing you hold the whole world.

—*Orhan Pamuk, Turkish novelist and screenwriter,* Snow

HAPPINESS

DAY 109

Good moms have dirty laundry, sticky floors, mis-matched socks, tired eyes, happy kids, and unlimited love.

—*Vanessa Barker, American writer and blogger*

DAY 110

A woman is the full circle. Within her is the power to create, nurture, and transform.

—*Diane Mariechild, author*

STRENGTH

Being a mother is an attitude,
not a biological relation.

—*Robert A. Heinlein, American writer,*
Have Space Suit—Will Travel

Just living is not enough . . . one must have sunshine, freedom, and a little flower.

—*Hans Christian Andersen, Danish author*

BEAUTY

To acquire knowledge, one must study; but to acquire wisdom, one must observe.

—*Marilyn vos Savant, American author and columnist*

WISDOM

LOVE

DAY 114

Some are kissing mothers and some are scolding mothers, but it is love just the same.

—*Pearl S. Buck, American writer and novelist*

Motherhood has taught me the meaning of living in the moment and being at peace. Children don't think about yesterday, and they don't think about tomorrow. They just exist in the moment.

—*Jessalyn Gilsig, Canadian actress*

HAPPINESS

DAY 116

My mother didn't specialize in home decor or gourmet cooking, and she didn't lift weights or run marathons. But she makes me feel like I am the most important, wonderful person ever born. If I could pick any mother in the whole world, it would be my mom.

—*April Perry, American co-founder of Power of Moms,* Motherhood Realized

STRENGTH

Strength does not come from physical capacity. It comes from an indomitable will.

—*Mahatma Gandhi, leader of Indian independence movement*

A family can develop only with a loving woman as its center.

—*Karl Wilhelm Friedrich Schlegel, German poet, literary critic, and philosopher*

RELATIONSHIPS

DAY 119

If we want to discover the full potential in our humanity, we need to celebrate those heartbreaking strengths and those glorious disabilities we all have. It is our humanity and all the potential within it that makes us beautiful.

—*Aimee Mullins, American athlete, actress, and fashion model*

DAY 120

One good mother
is worth a hundred
schoolmasters.

—*George Hebert, Welsh-born
English poet, orator, and priest*

WISDOM

DAY 121

Love yourself first and everything else falls into line. You really have to love yourself to get anything done in this world.

—*Lucille Ball, American comedian, actress, and model*

I want to be a fun mom. Not a gasping-for-air mom.

—Mariska Hargitay, American actress

HAPPINESS

STEWARDSHIP

DAY 123

You may have tangible wealth untold, caskets of jewels and coffers of gold. Richer than I you can never be—I had a mother who read to me.

—*Strickland Gillilan,
American poet and humorist*

By starting where you are, focusing on your strengths, and doing what you love to do, it becomes easier to let go of the irrelevant or ill-fitting expectations and standards you've developed over the years and create your own definition of what it means to be a good mom. When you start where you are, you put the past in its place and allow yourself to experience success little by little. When you focus on the things you're already good at, you get a boost of confidence that encourages you to learn new things. And when you do what you love to do, you usually do it well, creating a sense of contentment as well as energy for the less enjoyable things that still need to get done. You can't go wrong!

—*Allyson Reynolds, American writer,* Motherhood Realized

STRENGTH

There is no greater good in all the world than motherhood. The influence of a mother in the lives of her children is beyond calculation.

—*James E. Faust, religious leader, lawyer, and politician*

Youth is happy because it has the ability to see beauty. Anyone who keeps the ability to see beauty never grows old.

—*Franz Kafka, German-speaking Czech author*

BEAUTY

Mother is the one we count on
for the things that matter most
of all.

—*Katharine Butler Hathaway,*
American writer

WISDOM

DAY 128

Love is a better teacher than duty.

—*Albert Einstein, German-born theoretical physicist*

LOVE

DAY 129

Remember that happiness is a way of travel, not a destination.

—*Roy Goodman, American politician*

There is no way to be a perfect mother, and
a million ways to be a good one.

—Jill Churchill, American author

STEWARDSHIP

Where there is no struggle,
there is no strength.

*—Oprah Winfrey, American talk
show host and philanthropist*

STRENGTH

You have nothing in this world more precious than your children. When you grow old, when your hair turns white and your body grows weary, when you are prone to sit in a rocker and meditate on the things in your life, nothing will be so important as the question of how your children have turned out . . . Do not trade your birthright as a mother for some bauble of passing value . . . The baby you hold in your arms will grow quickly as the sunrise and the sunset of the rushing days.

—*Gordon B. Hinckley, American author and religious leader*

Happiness and confidence are
the prettiest things you can wear.

—*Taylor Swift, American singer-
songwriter and actress*

This whole thing, being a mom, isn't about me teaching my children. They're here to teach me.

—*Natalie Ellis, American writer,* Deliberate Motherhood

WISDOM

DAY 135

Our greatest duty to our children is to love
them first. Secondly, it is to teach them.
Not to frighten, force, or intimidate our
children into submission, but to effectively
teach them so that they have the knowledge and tools to govern themselves.

—*Richelle E. Goodrich, American author*

DAY 136

Let us be grateful to the people who make us happy; they are the charming gardeners who make our souls blossom.

—*Marcel Proust, French novelist*

Of all the roles I've played,
none has been as fulfilling
as being a mother.

—*Annette Funicello, American
actress and singer*

STEWARDSHIP

Strength doesn't come from what you can do. It comes from overcoming the things you once thought you couldn't do.

—*Rikki Rogers, writer*

DAY 139

All that I am or ever hope to
be, I owe to my angel mother.

—*Abraham Lincoln, former president
of the United States*

The sweetest sounds to mortals given
are heard in Mother, Home, and Heaven.

—*William Goldsmith Brown, poet*

BEAUTY

I have just three things to teach: simplicity, patience, compassion. These three are your greatest treasures.

—*Lao Tzu, Chinese philosopher and author*

WISDOM

She is the creature of life, the giver of life, and the giver of abundant love, care, and protection. Such are the great qualities of a mother. The bond between a mother and her child is the only real and purest bond in the world, the only true love we can ever find in our lifetime.

—*Ama H. Vanniarachchy, Sri Lankan author*

LOVE

When you're having dinner with your kids and your husband and someone says something funny or you're dying laughing because your three-year-old made a fart joke, it doesn't matter what else is going on. That's real happiness.

—Gwyneth Paltrow, American actress

HAPPINESS

This is what we do, my mother's life said. We find ourselves in the sacrifices we make.

—*Cammie McGovern, American author,* Neighborhood Watch

STEWARDSHIP

DAY 145

The best protection any woman can have is courage.

—*Elizabeth Cady Stanton, American suffragist, activist, and abolitionist*

RELATIONSHIPS

I think that the best thing we can do for our children is to allow them to do things for themselves, allow them to be strong, allow them to experience life on their own terms, allow them to take the subway . . . let them be better people, let them believe more in themselves.

—C. JoyBell C., *American writer, poet, and photographer*

DAY 147

Life is full of beauty. Notice it. Notice the bumble bee, the small child, and the smiling faces. Smell the rain, and feel the wind. Live your life to the fullest potential, and fight for your dreams.

—*Ashley Smith, American writer*

Don't listen to anyone's advice.
Listen to your baby . . . There
are so many books, doctors, and
well-meaning friends and family.
We like to say, "You don't need
a book. Your baby is a book. Just
pick it up and read it."

—*Mayim Bialik, American actress and
neuroscientist*

WISDOM

Spread love everywhere
you go. Let no one ever
come to you without
leaving happier.

—*Mother Teresa, Roman
Catholic religious sister and
missionary*

LOVE

Whatever it is we feel we are lacking, can we collectively decide—as deliberate mothers—that we are not going to sit around feeling discouraged about all the things we're not? Can we remind each other that it is our uniqueness and love that our children long for?

It is our voices. Our smiles. Our jiggly tummies. Of course we want to learn, improve, exercise, cook better, make our homes lovelier, and provide beautiful experiences for our children, but at the end of the day, our children don't want a discouraged, stressed-out mom who is wishing she were someone else.

If you ever find yourself looking in the mirror at a woman who feels badly that she hasn't yet made flower-shaped soap, please offer her this helpful reminder: "Your children want you!"

—*April Perry, American co-founder of Power of Moms,* Motherhood Realized

HAPPINESS

Mother is one to whom
you hurry when you
are troubled.

—*Emily Dickinson,
American poet*

STEWARDSHIP

DAY 152

Failure is the opportunity to begin again more intelligently.

—*Henry Ford, American industrialist and founder of the Ford Motor Company*

DAY 153

A mother never quite leaves her children at home, even when she doesn't take them along.

—*Margaret Culkin Banning, American author*

DAY 154

Your outer beauty will capture
the eyes; your inner beauty will
capture the heart.

—*Steven Aitchison, American writer*

WISDOM

The greatest lesson Mom ever taught me, though, was this one: She told me there would be times in your life when you have to choose between being loved and being respected. She said to always pick being respected, that love without respect was always fleeting—but that respect could grow into real, lasting love.

—*Chris Christie, American politician*

A mother's arms are made of tenderness, and children sleep soundly in them.

—*Victor Hugo, French novelist and poet*

LOVE

Sing out loud in the car, even, or especially, if it embarrasses your children.

—*Marilyn Penland, American author*

HAPPINESS

DAY 158

I thought my mom's whole purpose was to be my mom. That's how she made me feel.

—*Natasha Gregson Wagner, American actress*

DAY 159

Success is not final, failure is not fatal: it is the courage to continue that counts.

—*Winston Churchill, former prime minister of the United Kingdom*

Having children just puts the whole world into perspective. Everything else just disappears.

—*Kate Winslet, English actress and singer*

RELATIONSHIPS

Most of all the other beautiful things in life come by twos and threes, by dozens and hundreds. Plenty of roses, stars, sunsets, rainbows, brothers and sisters, aunts and cousins, comrades and friends—but only one mother in the whole world.

—*Kate Douglas Wiggin, American educator and author*

[My mother] used to say, "It takes the same energy to think small as to think big." Whenever I went to her, thinking one way about something, she'd say, "Bigger." Whatever I wanted out of life, she'd say, "Bigger." I grew up wanting a little bit more. I was taught to aim high.

—*Daymond John, American entrepreneur*

WISDOM

DAY 163

Mama was my greatest teacher—a teacher of compassion, love, and fearlessness. If love is sweet as a flower, then my mother is that sweet flower of love.

—*Stevie Wonder, American musician and producer*

DAY 164

I don't think that there are any limits to how excellent we could make life seem.

—*Jonathan Safran Foer, American writer,* Everything Is Illuminated

HAPPINESS

STEWARDSHIP

Motherhood is not a hobby; it is a calling. It is not something to do if you can squeeze the time in; it is what God gave you time for.

—*Rachel Jankovic,*
American author
and blogger

DAY 166

The hand that rocks the cradle is
the hand that rules the world.

—*W. R. Wallace, American poet*

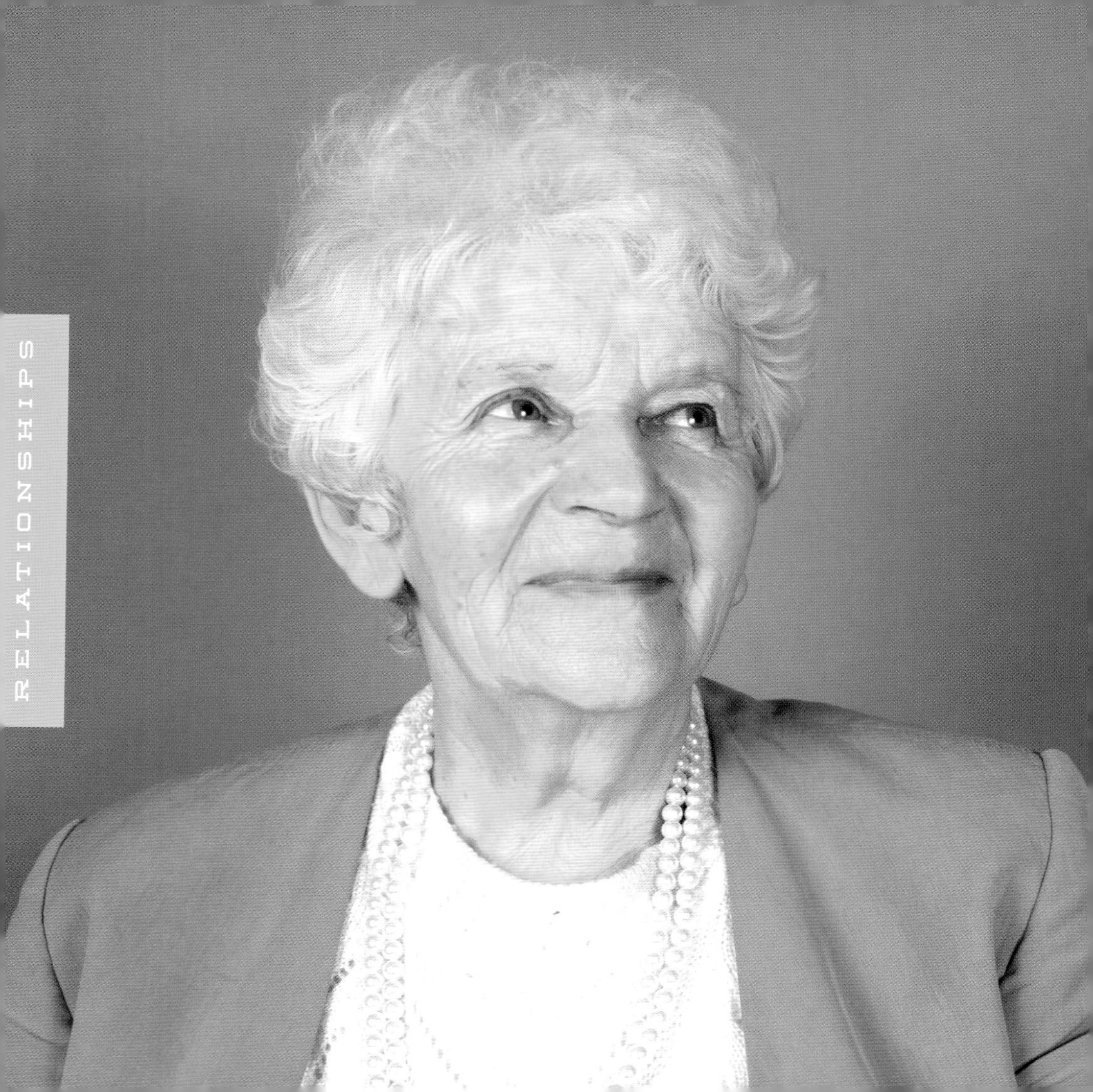

DAY 167

My mother . . . she is beautiful, softened at the edges and tempered with a spine of steel. I want to grow old and be like her.

—*Jodi Picoult, American author*

DAY 168

Some people, no matter how old they get, never lose their beauty—they merely move it from their faces into their hearts.

—*Martin Buxbaum, American poet, author, and editor*

BEAUTY

My mother is my root, my foundation. She planted the seed that I base my life on, and that is the belief that the ability to achieve starts in your mind.

—*Michael Jordan, former professional basketball player*

WISDOM

If you can learn to love
yourself and all the flaws,
you can love other people
so much better. And that
makes you so happy.

—*Kristin Chenoweth, American
actress and singer*

LOVE

HAPPINESS

For every minute you are angry, you lose sixty seconds of happiness.

—*Ralph Waldo Emerson, American essayist, lecturer, and poet*

Motherhood is a choice you make every
day, to put someone else's happiness and
well-being ahead of your own, to teach
the hard lessons, to do the right thing even
when you're not sure what the right thing
is . . . and to forgive yourself, over and over
again, for doing everything wrong.

—*Donna Ball, American novelist,* At Home on
Ladybug Farm

STEWARDSHIP

The most common way people give up their power is by thinking they don't have any.

—*Alice Walker, American author*

STRENGTH

There is also comfort in knowing that our children are blissfully ignorant of our so-called inadequacies—they think we're perfect just the way we are . . . They don't see our cellulite, our deflated bank accounts, our cluttered closets, let alone our undeserved self-loathing. All they see is their mother: the woman who takes care of them, feeds them, hugs them, listens to them, *loves* them. When you inevitably feel unqualified for the task at hand . . . remind yourself that motherhood is ultimately about your children, and they think you are wonderful!

—*Allyson Reynolds, American writer,* Deliberate Motherhood

RELATIONSHIPS

Mother: the most beautiful word on the lips of mankind.

—*Kahlil Gibran, Lebanese-American artist, poet, and writer*

BEAUTY

DAY 176

This mothering role will teach you more about yourself than you ever expected.

—*Tricia Goyer, American author,* Teen Mom: You're Stronger Than You Think

DAY 177

A mother is the one who fills your heart in the first place.

—Amy Tan, Chinese-American writer and novelist, Saving Fish from Drowning

DAY 178

Taking joy in living is a woman's best cosmetic.

—*Rosalind Russell, American actress*

DAY 179

The phrase "working mother" is redundant.

—*Jane Sellman, American author and professor*

The brick walls are there for a reason.
The brick walls are not there to keep us
out. The brick walls are there to give us
a chance to show how badly we want
something. Because the brick walls
are there to stop the people who don't
want it badly enough. They're there to
stop the other people.

— *Randy Pausch, American professor and author*

STRENGTH

DAY 181

Mothers hold their children's hands for a short while, but their hearts forever.

—*Unknown*

DAY 182

My mother is a poem I'll never be able to write, though everything I write is a poem to my mother.

—*Sharon Doubiago, American poet*

DAY 183

A loving heart is the truest wisdom.

—*Charles Dickens, English writer and social critic*

DAY 184

There's nothing like a
mama-hug.

—*Terri Guillemets, American
quotation anthologist*

LOVE

DAY 185

A pessimist is one who makes difficulties of his opportunities and an optimist is one who makes opportunities of his difficulties.

—*Harry S. Truman, former president of the United States*

Mothers always worry.
There's no off switch.

—*Priscille Sibley, American author and poet,* The Promise of Stardust

STEWARDSHIP

DAY 187

Mothers possess a power beyond
that of a king on his throne.

—*Mabel Hale, American author*

DAY 188

Mirror, mirror on
the wall, I am my
mother after all.

—*Unknown*

Beauty is not in the face;
beauty is a light in the
heart.

—*Kahlil Gibran, Lebanese-
American artist, poet, and writer*

BEAUTY

My mother said the cure for thinking too much about yourself was helping somebody who was worse off than you.

—Sylvia Plath, American poet, novelist, and short story writer, The Bell Jar

WISDOM

Before you were conceived, I wanted you. Before you were born, I loved you. Before you were an hour, I would die for you. This is the miracle of love.

—*Maureen Hawkins, author*

LOVE

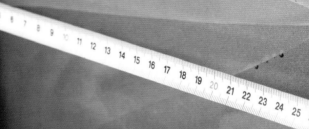

DAY 192

Happiness is not the absence of problems; it's the ability to deal with them.

—*Steve Maraboli, speaker, author, and behavioral science academic,* Life, the Truth, and Being Free

DAY 193

Motherhood is hard. It's demanding,
painful, and often unappreciated. But
the satisfaction I feel as a mother—
even on the longest, most discouraging,
exhausting days—far exceeds what I
ever expected out of family life.

—*April Perry, American co-founder of Power of
Moms,* Motherhood Realized

DAY 194

———

When we do the best we can, we never know what miracle is wrought in our life, or in the life of another.

—*Helen Keller, American author, political activist, and lecturer*

Make a memory with your children,
spend some time to show you care;
toys and trinkets can't replace those
precious moments that you share.

—*Elaine Hardt, American blogger and writer*

RELATIONSHIPS

DAY 196

In nature, nothing is perfect and everything
is perfect. Trees can be contorted, bent in
weird ways, and they're still beautiful.

DAY 197

That best academy, a mother's knee.

—*James Russell Lowell,*
poet, critic, and diplomat

WISDOM

Because I feel that, in the Heavens above,

The angels, whispering to one another,

Can find, among their burning terms of love,

None so devotional as that of "Mother."

—*Edgar Allan Poe, American author, poet, editor, and literary critic*

LOVE

DAY 199

They say a person needs just three things to be truly happy in this world: someone to love, something to do, and something to hope for.

—*Tom Bodett, American author, voice actor, and radio host*

There is no one perfect way to be a good mother. Each situation is unique. Each mother has different challenges, different skills and abilities, and certainly different children. The choice is different and unique for each mother and each family.

—*M. Russell Ballard, American author and religious leader*

STEWARDSHIP

STRENGTH

DAY 201

Do what you can, with what you have, where you are.

—*Theodore Roosevelt, former president of the United States*

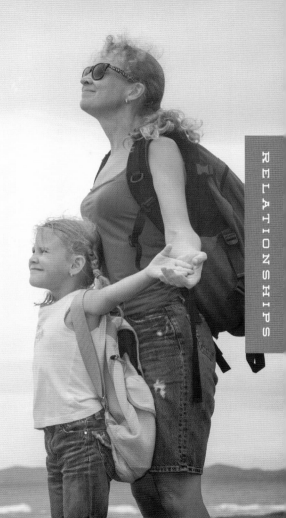

In a child's eyes, a mother is a goddess. She can be glorious or terrible, benevolent or filled with wrath, but she commands love either way. I am convinced that this is the greatest power in the universe.

—*N. K. Jemisin, American writer and blogger,* The Hundred Thousand Kingdoms

RELATIONSHIPS

DAY 203

To be pregnant is to be vitally alive, thoroughly woman, and distressingly inhabited. Soul and spirit are stretched—along with the body—making pregnancy a time of transition, growth, and profound beginnings.

—*Anne Christian Buchanan, American author*

DAY 204

Think big thoughts but
relish small pleasures.

—*H. Jackson Brown Jr., American
author*

LOVE

Sometimes when you pick up your child you can feel the map of your own bones beneath your hands, or smell the scent of your skin in the nape of his neck. This is the most extraordinary thing about motherhood—finding a piece of yourself separate and apart that all the same you could not live without.

—*Jodi Picoult, American author,* Perfect Match

My mom is a never-ending
song in my heart of comfort,
happiness, and being. I may
sometimes forget the words,
but I always remember the
tune.

—*Graycie Harmon, American author*

HAPPINESS

Behind every great
kid is a mom who's
pretty sure she's
screwing it up.

—*Anonymous*

STEWARDSHIP

Perseverance: secret of all triumphs.

—*Victor Hugo, French novelist and poet*

STRENGTH

If you want your children to turn out well, spend twice as much time with them and half as much money.

—*Abigail Van Buren, American advice columnist*

RELATIONSHIPS

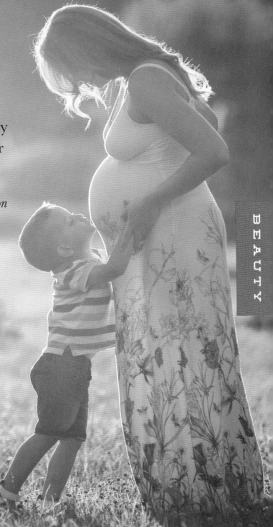

Pregnancy and motherhood are the most beautiful and significantly life-altering events that I have ever experienced.

—Elisabeth Hasselbeck, American television personality and talk show host

BEAUTY

DAY 211

It is not what you do for your children, but what you have taught them to do for themselves, that will make them successful human beings.

Ann Landers, American advice columnist

Grown don't mean nothing to a mother. A child is a child. They get bigger, older, but grown? What's that suppose to mean? In my heart, it don't mean a thing.

—*Toni Morrison, American novelist, editor, and professor,* Beloved

LOVE

Children are happy
because they don't have a
file in their minds called
"All the Things That
Could Go Wrong."

—Marianne Williamson,
American spiritual activist,
author, and lecturer

HAPPINESS

A mother is she who can take the place of all others, but whose place no one else can take.

—*Gaspard Mermillod,*
Swiss Cardinal of the
Roman Catholic Church

STEWARDSHIP

The strength of motherhood is greater than natural laws.

—*Barbara Kingsolver, American novelist, essayist, and poet*

STRENGTH

There is a rhythm to motherhood. Some moments call for an upbeat tempo, others are more like a march, and still others wind about at a soothing crawl. At times, we dictate the rhythm, and our families dance in step with the beat we set. Other times, our children's rhythm out-sings our own, and we fall in line with the beat of their drums. Being in tune with the rhythm of your family and your rhythm as a mother is essential to finding balance.

—*Jennifer Cummings, American writer,*
Deliberate Motherhood

RELATIONSHIPS

BEAUTY

DAY 217

You create beauty with your attitude, your behavior, your actions. It's all up to you.

——*Unknown*

Mothers were the only ones you could depend on to tell the whole, unvarnished truth.

——*Margaret Dilloway, Japanese-American author,* How to Be an American Housewife

WISDOM

A mother's arms are more comforting than anyone else's.

—*Princess Diana, late princess of Wales*

LOVE

Happiness cannot be traveled to, owned, earned, or worn. It is the spiritual experience of living every minute with love, grace, and gratitude.

—*Denis Waitley, American motivational speaker and author*

HAPPINESS

STEWARDSHIP

Nobody knows of the work it makes

To keep the home together.

Nobody knows of the steps it takes,

Nobody knows but Mother.

—*Anonymous*

Motherhood brings as much joy as ever, but it still brings boredom, exhaustion, and sorrow, too. Nothing else ever will make you as happy or as sad, as proud or as tired, for nothing is quite as hard as helping a person develop his own individuality, especially while you struggle to keep your own.

—*Marguerite Kelly and Elia Parsons, American authors,* The Mother's Almanac

STRENGTH

DAY 223

We all carry our mothers inside us.

Katherine Center,
American author, Things to
Remember Not to Forget

You are imperfect, permanently and
inevitably flawed. And you are beautiful.

—*Amy Bloom, American author*

BEAUTY

The mother's heart is the child's schoolroom.

—*Henry Ward Beecher, American Congregationalist clergyman*

WISDOM

My mother had a slender, small body,
but a large heart—a heart so large that
everybody's joys found welcome in it,
and hospitable accommodation.

—*Mark Twain, American author and humorist*

LOVE

DAY 227

People are just as happy as they make up their minds to be.

—*Abraham Lincoln, former president of the United States*

I cannot forget my mother. She is my bridge. When I needed to get across, she steadied herself long enough for me to run across safely.

—Renita Weems, American writer

STEWARDSHIP

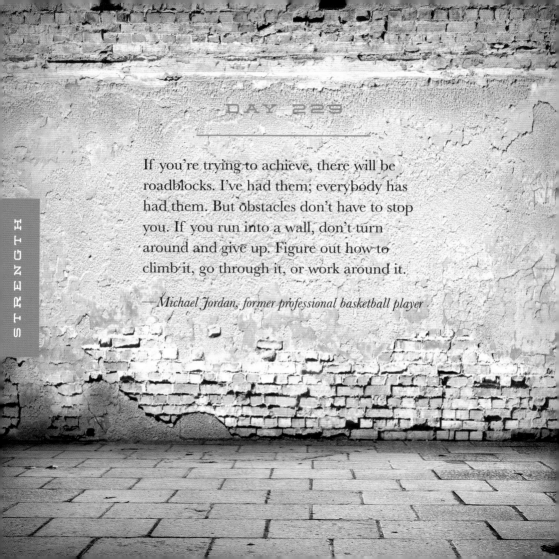

STRENGTH

DAY 229

If you're trying to achieve, there will be roadblocks. I've had them; everybody has had them. But obstacles don't have to stop you. If you run into a wall, don't turn around and give up. Figure out how to climb it, go through it, or work around it.

—*Michael Jordan, former professional basketball player*

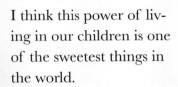

I think this power of living in our children is one of the sweetest things in the world.

—*Louisa May Alcott, American novelist,* Jo's Boys

RELATIONSHIPS

Life is good. Life is a gift. Life is precious.

Don't let the mundane moments in life rob you of the beauty of normal that surrounds you. Remind yourself to look for the beauty, the gems that are tucked within the fabric of the everyday normal. Force yourself to wake up, to see, to remember, and to be thankful for the blessings that fill your life.

Don't lose sight of the good.

—*Rachel Martin, American writer,* Motherhood Realized

BEAUTY

My mother was the most beautiful woman I ever saw. All I am I owe to my mother. I attribute my success in life to the moral, intellectual, and physical education I received from her.

—*George Washington, first president of the United States*

WISDOM

Being a full-time mother is one of the highest salaried jobs . . . since the payment is pure love.

—*Mildred B. Vermont,*
author

LOVE

One of the things I learned the hard way was that it doesn't pay to get discouraged. Keeping busy and making optimism a way of life can restore your faith in yourself.

—*Lucille Ball, American comedian, actress, and model*

HAPPINESS

Isn't this the truth of any good mother? That in all of our lives, we worry only about those we brought into this world, regardless of whether they loved us back or treated us fairly or understood our shortcomings.

—*Adriana Trigiani, American novelist, television writer, producer, and film director,* Big Cherry Holler

Perhaps it takes courage to
raise children.

—*John Steinbeck, American author,*
East of Eden

STRENGTH

RELATIONSHIPS

Mothers, I believe, intoxicate us. We idolize them and take them for granted. We hate them and blame them and exalt them more thoroughly than anyone else in our lives. We sift through the evidence of their love, reassure ourselves of their affection and its biological genesis. We can steal and lie and leave and they will love us.

—*Megan Mayhew Bergman, American writer,* Birds of a Lesser Paradise: Stories

Art is the child of nature in whom we trace the features of the mother's face.

—*Henry Wadsworth Longfellow,*
American poet and educator

WISDOM

Use what talents you possess;
the woods would be very
silent if no birds sang there
except those that sang best.

—*Henry Van Dyke, American
author, educator, and clergyman*

Every bit of patience I show is a measure of love that will be etched in their hearts forever. They may not remember the exact incident, but they will remember the color of my love—a soft, safe color that I hope is painted in their memories forever.

—*Natalie Ellis, American writer,* Deliberate Motherhood

LOVE

DAY 241

I am determined to be cheerful and happy in whatever situation I may find myself. For I have learned that the greater part of our misery or unhappiness is determined not by our circumstance, but by our disposition.

—*Martha Washington, first First Lady of the United States*

There are some things that
only a mother can do.

—*Anonymous*

STEWARDSHIP

STRENGTH

Courage is being
scared to death—but
saddling up anyway.

—*John Wayne, American
actor*

A little girl, asked where her home was,
replied, "Where mother is."

—*Keith L. Brooks, American author*

RELATIONSHIPS

BEAUTY

DAY 245

Beauty is how you feel inside, and it reflects in your eyes.

—*Sophia Loren, Italian actress*

And despite everything I know now, I still believe, as I did when I was little, that there is an entire universe of things my mother knows that I don't.

—*Katherine Center, American author,* Things to Remember Not to Forget

WISDOM

A mother's love is patient
and forgiving when all others
are forsaking; it never fails or
falters, even though the heart
is breaking.

—*Helen Steiner Rice, American writer*

LOVE

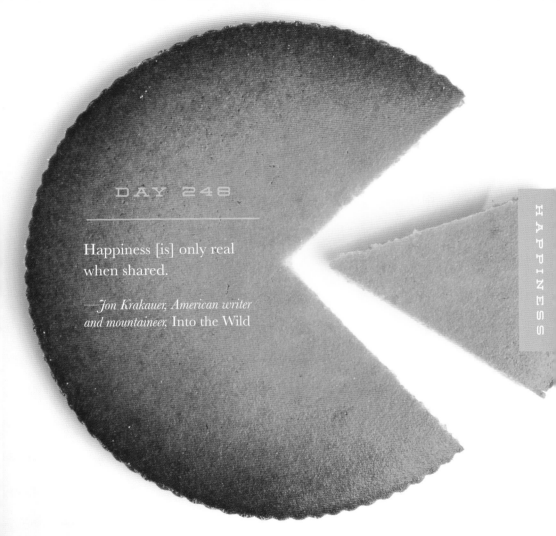

Happiness [is] only real
when shared.

*—Jon Krakauer, American writer
and mountaineer,* Into the Wild

HAPPINESS

DAY 249

There's absolutely no sort of acknowledgement or reward for this—except for the intangible of my kids growing up to be wonderful people.

—*Jodie Foster, American actress, director, and producer*

No one can make you feel inferior without your consent.

—*Eleanor Roosevelt, former First Lady of the United States, activist, and diplomat*

STRENGTH

DAY 251

To a child's ear, "mother" is
magic in any language.

—*Arlene Benedict, author*

A mother is always the beginning. She is how things begin.

—*Amy Tan, Chinese-American writer and novelist,* The Bonesetter's Daughter

WISDOM

I love my mother for all the times she said absolutely nothing . . . Thinking back on it all, it must have been the most difficult part of mothering she ever had to do: knowing the outcome, yet feeling she had no right to keep me from charting my own path. I thank her for all her virtues, but mostly for never once having said, "I told you so."

—*Erma Bombeck, American humorist and columnist*

Love is that condition in which the happiness of another person is essential to your own.

—*Robert A. Heinlein, American writer,* Stranger in a Strange Land

LOVE

DAY 255

The more you praise and celebrate your life, the more there is
in life to celebrate.

—*Oprah Winfrey, American talk show
host and philanthropist*

Sorry to say, women run the house. They run the family. They hold things up. I mean, it's like you don't ever see your mom get sick because she handles everything. And it's kind of amazing, I think, to show people just how strong women are.

—*Sophia Bush, American actress, director, spokesperson, and activist*

STEWARDSHIP

STRENGTH

Your time is limited, so don't waste it living someone else's life. Don't be trapped by dogma—which is living with the results of other people's thinking. Don't let the noise of other's opinions drown out your own inner voice. And most important, have the courage to follow your heart and intuition. They somehow already know what you truly want to become. Everything else is secondary.

—*Steve Jobs, American entrepreneur, marketer, and inventor*

Becoming a mother makes you the mother of all children. From now on each wounded, abandoned, frightened child is yours. You live in the suffering mothers of every race and creed and weep with them. You long to comfort all who are desolate.

—*Charlotte Gray, British-born Canadian historian and author*

RELATIONSHIPS

BEAUTY

DAY 259

Still the most magical day of my
life is the day I became a mom.

—*Linda Becker, author*

If a child is not listening, don't despair. Time and truth are on your side. At the right moment, your words will return as if from heaven itself. Your testimony will never leave your children.

—*Neil L. Andersen, religious leader and author*

WISDOM

When you look into your mother's eyes, you know that is the purest love you can find on this earth.

—*Mitch Albom, American author, radio and television broadcaster, and musician,* For One More Day

LOVE

In order to carry a positive action, we must develop here a positive vision.

—*Dalai Lama, Tibetan Buddhist and spiritual leader*

HAPPINESS

STEWARDSHIP

I once read a book called *The Sacrificial Mother* by Carin Ruben-stein, which describes many mothers who sacrifice pretty much all of themselves for the sake of their children. For example, they dress their children in designer clothes and provide them with lessons of all kinds, yet they dress themselves in old sweats and never take time to do things they enjoy. Over time, this habit leads to depression and frustration, and often the sacrifi-cial mothers simply want a way out.

We know that if we really want to have the stamina, enthusi-asm, and patience to raise great children, we need to take care of ourselves first. The common airplane/oxygen mask analogy applies here: you put the mask on yourself so you can then care for your little ones. Underneath the title of "Mommy" is a real, live lady with her own name, who is just as important as everyone else.

There are certainly times when sacrifice is necessary and noble. We give up sleep for the sake of our newborns or sick children, we let the house get messier than we'd like it so our children can play and enjoy the excitement of childhood, we give our children the last grape popsicle (even though that's our favorite flavor) because their eyes light up when they see the color purple. Each of us has benefited from the sacrifice of a mother, and we are dedicated to sacrificing for our own children. But throughout all this, we need to believe that we are of value as women as *people*.

—*April Perry, American co-founder of Power of Moms,* Motherhood Realized

DAY 264

If you're going through hell, keep going.

—*Winston Churchill, former prime minister of the United Kingdom*

That's the strange thing about being a mother: until you have a baby, you don't even realize how much you were missing one.

—*Jodi Picoult, American author,* Vanishing Acts

RELATIONSHIPS

What you do, the way you think, makes you beautiful.

—*Scott Westerfeld, American writer,*
Uglies

BEAUTY

DAY 267

She openeth her mouth with
wisdom; and in her tongue is
the law of kindness.

—Proverbs 31:26

DAY 268

I will protect you until you are grown, and then I will let you fly free. But loving you, that is for always.

—Charlotte Gray, British-born Canadian historian and author

LOVE

HAPPINESS

Even if I'm setting myself up for failure, I think it's worth trying to be a mother who delights in who her children are, in their knock-knock jokes and earnest questions. A mother who spends less time obsessing about what will happen, or what has happened, and more time reveling in what is. A mother who doesn't fret over failings and slights, who realizes her worries and anxieties are just thoughts, the continuous chattering and judgement of a too busy mind. A mother who doesn't worry so much about being bad or good but just recognizes that she's both, and neither. A mother who does her best, and for whom that is good enough, even if, in the end, her best turns out to be, simply, not bad.

—*Ayelet Waldman, Israeli-American writer,* Bad Mother: A Chronicle of Maternal Crimes, Minor Calamities, and Occasional Moments of Grace

By the proverbial standards of the world, it's easy to classify the majority of mothers, by virtue of what we do, day in and day out, as ordinary. But make sure you don't forget to use the word "fabulous" in front of that description.

Here's to being fabulously ordinary!

—*Tiffany Sowby, American writer,* Motherhood Realized

STEWARDSHIP

DAY 271

Accept responsibility for your life.
Know that it is you who will get you
where you want to go, no one else.

—*Les Brown, American motivational speaker,*
host, and author

The tie which links mother and child is of such pure and immaculate strength as to be never violated.

—*Washington Irving, American author and essayist*

RELATIONSHIPS

DAY 273

I've learned the value of absorbing the moment. I remember the first time [my daughter] saw her shadow. My God, it was like shadows had just been invented. It was the most exquisite moment.

—*Thandie Newton, English actress*

My mom was always saying: "Be whatever you want to be, but stick with it. Don't waver. Don't change who you are for anybody."

—*Miranda Lambert, American country music artist*

WISDOM

LOVE

Because even if the whole world was throwing rocks at you, if you had your mother at your back, you'd be okay. Some deep-rooted part of you would know you were loved. That you deserved to be loved.

—*Jojo Moyes, British journalist and novelist,* One Plus One

Happiness is not something ready-made. It comes from your own actions.

—*Dalai Lama XIV*

HAPPINESS

Put [your daughter] to sleep yourself every night. Sing to her and cradle her in your arms and sit by her side—every night. Because one day you won't be able to, and it's going to happen really fast.

—*Salma Hayek, Mexican-American actress, director, and producer*

STEWARDSHIP

You have to have confidence in your ability,
and then be tough enough to follow through.

—*Rosalynn Carter, former First Lady of the United
States*

STRENGTH

DAY 279

Mothers and their children are in a category all their own. There's no bond so strong in the entire world. No love so instantaneous and forgiving.

—*Gail Tsukiyama,*
American novelist,
Dreaming Water

The future belongs to those who believe in the beauty of their dreams.

—*Eleanor Roosevelt, former First Lady of the United States, activist, and diplomat*

BEAUTY

[My mother] had handed down respect for
the possibilities—and the will to grasp them.

—*Alice Walker, American author*

WISDOM

DAY 282

Life began with waking up and loving my mother's face.

—*George Eliot, English novelist*

LOVE

HAPPINESS

The pain and joy of motherhood go hand in hand. They are inseparable. You can't get the baby without the waves of labor pains. You can't become the strong and patient and knowledge-able mother you want to be or raise the resilient and wonderful children you dream of without the waves of trials and joy that stretch and grow you and bind hearts together.

So when that next motherhood pain hits you, remember: "Envision your-self on the ocean, riding the waves up and down, letting them wash over you, accepting the ups and downs as part of a beautiful process."

—*Saren Eyre Loosli, co-founder of Power of Moms*, Motherhood Realized

More than in any other human relationship, overwhelmingly more, motherhood means being instantly interruptible, responsive, and responsible.

—*Tillie Olsen, American writer*

STEWARDSHIP

DAY 285

Being deeply loved by someone gives you strength, while loving someone deeply gives you courage.

—*Lao-Tzu, Chinese philosopher and poet*

Being a mother is not about what you gave up to have a child, but what you've gained from having one.

—*Unknown*

RELATIONSHIPS

BEAUTY

The significance of the cherry blossom tree in Japanese culture goes back hundreds of years. In their country, the cherry blossom represents the fragility and the beauty of life. It's a reminder that life is almost overwhelmingly beautiful but that it is also tragically short.

—*Homaro Cantu, American chef and inventor*

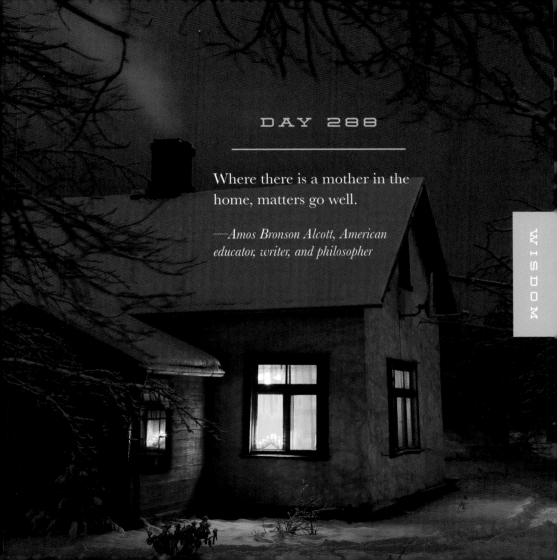

Where there is a mother in the home, matters go well.

—*Amos Bronson Alcott, American educator, writer, and philosopher*

WISDOM

Blessed is a mother that would give up part of her soul for her children's happiness.

—*Shannon L. Alder, American author*

LOVE

There is only one way to happiness and that is to cease worrying about things which are beyond the power of our will.

—*Epictetus, Greek Stoic philosopher*

HAPPINESS

I've always been so apathetic. I figured, *OK, maybe the world is going to fall down around me.* Now I want to make a better world . . . that's motherhood.

—*Cass Elliot, American singer*

STEWARDSHIP

We don't develop courage by being happy every day. We develop it by surviving difficult times and challenging adversity.

—*Barbara de Angelis, American relationship consultant*

STRENGTH

DAY 293

All of those clichés—those things you hear about having a baby and motherhood—all of them are true. And all of them are the most beautiful things you will ever experience.

—*Penelope Cruz, Spanish actress and model*

When you are balanced and when you listen and attend to the needs of your body, mind, and spirit, your natural beauty comes out.

—*Christy Turlington, American model*

BEAUTY

A mother knows what her child's gone through, even if she didn't see it herself.

—*Pramoedya Ananta Toer,*
Indonesian author and historian

WISDOM

Love is the most powerful force
we have as mothers, yet how
often do we move through
our days without "putting our
hearts on"—forgetting to feel
and express the love that really
is at the core of all we do. . . .
When we perform our moth-
ering duties with love, rather
than resentment, the power
of that love changes, shapes,
and molds us—as much as it
changes, shapes, and molds our
children.

—*Saydi Shumway, American writer,*
Deliberate Motherhood

LOVE

HAPPINESS

DAY 297

Thousands of candles can be lighted from a single candle, and the life of the candle will not be shortened. Happiness never decreases by being shared.

—*the Buddha*

At the end of the day, the most overwhelming key to a child's success is the positive involvement of parents.

—*Jane D. Hull, American politician*

STEWARDSHIP

DAY 299

When we long for life without difficulties, remind us that oaks grow strong in contrary winds and diamonds are made under pressure.

—*Peter Marshall, American TV and radio personality*

What is a mom but the sunshine of our days and the north star of our nights.

—*Robert Brault, American author*

RELATIONSHIPS

DAY 301

Beauty is about perception, not about makeup. I think the beginning of all beauty is knowing and liking oneself. You can't put on makeup, or dress yourself, or do your hair with any sort of fun or joy if you're doing it from a position of correction.

—*Kevyn Aucoin, American make-up artist, photographer and author*

DAY 302

He who seeks truth shall find beauty. He who seeks beauty shall find vanity. He who seeks order shall find gratification. He who seeks gratification shall be disappointed. He who considers himself the servant of his fellow beings shall find the joy of self-expression. He who seeks self-expression shall fall into the pit of arrogance.

—*Moshe Safdie, Israeli-Canadian-American architect and author*

LOVE

One day I read a quote by Mother Teresa that stuck with me: "We can do no great things, only small things with great love."

Motherhood is perhaps the greatest example of a long, long string of small things that, done with great love and extra thought, can have ripple effects that go on for generations. Big things are MADE out of little things.

—*Saren Eyre Loosli, American co-founder of Power of Moms,* Motherhood Realized

HAPPINESS

DAY 304

If mama ain't happy, ain't nobody happy.

—*Anonymous*

STEWARDSHIP

Every word, facial expression, gesture, or action on the part of a parent gives the child some message about self-worth. It is sad that so many parents don't realize what messages they are sending.

—*Virginia Satir, American author and social worker*

DAY 306

Life has many ways of testing a person's will,
either by having nothing happen at all or by
having everything happen all at once.

—*Paulo Coelho, Brazilian lyricist and novelist*

RELATIONSHIPS

I remember my mother's prayers and they have always followed me. They have clung to me all my life.

—*Abraham Lincoln, former president of the United States*

DAY 308

Let the beauty of what you
love be what you do.

—*Rūmī, Persian poet, theologian,
and mystic*

The pessimist complains about the wind; the optimist expects it to change; the realist adjusts the sails.

—*William Arthur Ward, American writer*

WISDOM

DAY 310

Mother love is the fuel that enables a normal human being to do the impossible.

—*Marion C. Garretty, American author*

Happiness is not a matter of intensity but of balance, order, rhythm, and harmony.

—*Thomas Merton, American writer and mystic*

HAPPINESS

To be in your children's memories tomorrow, you have to be in their lives today.

—*Barbara Johnson, American author*

STEWARDSHIP

DAY 313

I know how to do any-
thing—I'm a mom.

—*Roseanne Barr, American
actress, comedian, and writer*

STRENGTH

There's something that just happens to you when you have a baby, and you look at their little eyes for the first time when you're holding them. They've been safe inside your belly for almost ten months, and now they're in your arms. Intuition kicks in, where you will do anything for them and you have all the tools inside of you to take care of them.

—*Hillary Duff, American actress and singer*

RELATIONSHIPS

DAY 315

Sometimes the most beautiful thing is precisely the one that comes unexpectedly and unearned, hence something given truly as a present.

—*Anna Freud, Austrian-born British psychoanalyist and last child of Sigmund Freud*

Always be a first-rate version of yourself instead of a second-rate version of somebody else.

—*Judy Garland, American singer, actress, and vaudevillian*

WISDOM

DAY 317

Whatever else is
unsure in this stinking
dunghill of a world, a
mother's love is not.

—*James Joyce, Irish
novelist and poet*

LOVE

Joy, rather than happiness, is the goal of life, for joy is the emotion which accompanies our fulfilling our natures as human beings. It is based on the experience of one's identity as a being of worth and dignity.

—Rollo May, American existential psychologist and author

HAPPINESS

STEWARDSHIP

DAY 319

Parenthood: it's about guiding the next generation and forgiving the last.

——*Peter Krause, American illustrator and comic book artist*

I believe this with all my heart: the greatest coach of all time in my eyes is my mom. She's instilled in me a toughness and a perseverance and just a never-quit mentality, and I thank her every day for providing that for me, for what she sacrificed her life for.

—Scott Brooks, American NBA basketball player and coach

STRENGTH

RELATIONSHIPS

What do girls do who haven't any mothers to help them through their troubles?

—*Louisa May Alcott,*
American novelist

DAY 322

Consider a tree for a moment. As beautiful as trees are to look at, we don't see what goes on underground— as they grow roots. Trees must develop deep roots in order to grow strong and produce their beauty. But we don't see the roots. We just see and enjoy the beauty. In much the same way, what goes on inside of us is like the roots of a tree.

—*Joyce Meyer, American Christian author and speaker*

A day of worry is more exhausting than a week of work.

—John Lubbock, English banker, Liberal politician, philanthropist

WISDOM

Love is the most terrible, and also the most generous of the passions; it is the only one which includes in its dreams the happiness of someone else.

—*Alphonse Karr, French critic, journalist, and novelist*

LOVE

DAY 325

[Motherhood is] the biggest gamble in the world. It is the glorious life force. It's huge and scary—it's an act of infinite optimism.

—*Gilda Radner, American comedian and actress*

STEWARDSHIP

DAY 326

It's not our job to toughen our children up to face a cruel and heartless world. It's our job to raise children who will make the world a little less cruel and heartless.

—*L. R. Knost,* Two Thousand Kisses a Day: Gentle Parenting Through the Ages and Stages

STRENGTH

If you can control your behavior when everything around you is out of control, you can model for your children a valuable lesson in patience and understanding . . . and snatch an opportunity to shape character.

—*Jane Clayson Johnson, American journalist and author*, I Am a Mother

A mother does not become pregnant in order to provide employment to medical people. Giving birth is an ecstatic, jubilant adventure not available to males. It is a woman's crowning creative experience of a lifetime.

—*John Stevenson, English author*

DAY 329

My theory on life is that life is beautiful. Life doesn't change. You have a day, and a night, and a month, and a year. We people change—we can be miserable or we can be happy. It's what you make of your life.

—*Mohammed bin Rashid Al Maktoum, Vice President and Prime Minister of the United Arab Emirates*

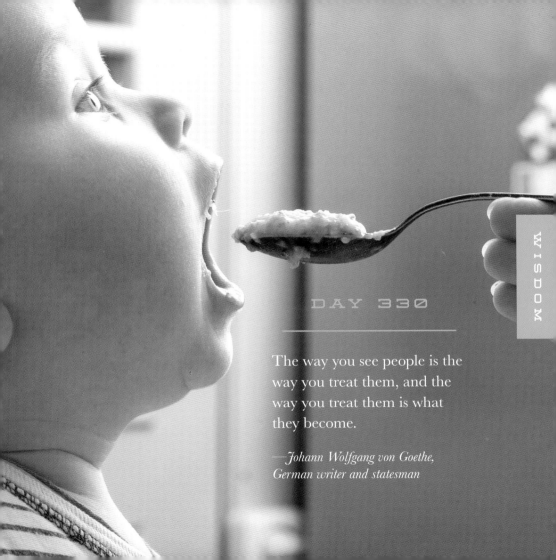

DAY 330

The way you see people is the way you treat them, and the way you treat them is what they become.

—*Johann Wolfgang von Goethe,*
German writer and statesman

LOVE

DAY 331

By loving them for more than their abilities we show our children that they are much more than the sum of their accomplishments.

—*Eileen Kennedy-Moore, American psychologist and author,* Smart Parenting for Smart Kids

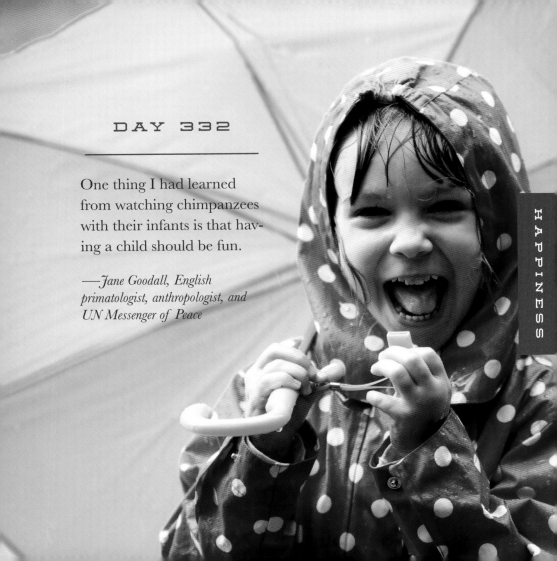

DAY 332

One thing I had learned
from watching chimpanzees
with their infants is that having a child should be fun.

—*Jane Goodall, English
primatologist, anthropologist, and
UN Messenger of Peace*

HAPPINESS

STEWARDSHIP

Children are gifts.
They are not ours for
the breaking. They are
ours for the making.

—*Dan Pearce, American
author,* Single Dad
Laughing

To describe my mother
would be to write about
a hurricane in its perfect
power.

—*Maya Angelou, American author
and poet*

STRENGTH

DAY 335

Being a parent is dirty and scary and beautiful and hard and miraculous and exhausting and thankless and joyful and frustrating all at once. It's everything.

—*Jill Smokler, American blogger and author,* Confessions of a Scary Mommy

The longer I live, the more beautiful life becomes.

—*Frank Lloyd Wright, American architect, writer, and educator*

BEAUTY

When you give yourself, you
receive more than you give.

—*Antoine de Saint-Exupery, French
aristocrat, poet, and pioneering aviator*

WISDOM

DAY 338

I will look after you and
I will look after anybody
you say needs to be
looked after, any way you
say. I am here. I brought
my whole self to you. I
am your mother.

—*Maya Angelou, American
author and poet,* Mom & Me
& Mom

LOVE

My children teach
me to slow down and
enjoy life. My children
are the reason I laugh,
smile, and want to get
up every morning.

—*Gena Lee Nolin,*
American actress and model

HAPPINESS

We can surely no longer pretend that our children are growing up into a peaceful, secure, and civilized world. We've come to the point where it's irresponsible to try to protect them from the irrational world they will have to live in when they grow up. The children themselves haven't yet isolated themselves by selfishness and indifference; they do not fall easily into the error of despair; they are considerably braver than most grownups. Our responsibility to them is not to pretend that if we don't look, evil will go away, but to give them weapons against it.

—*Madeleine L'Engle, American writer,* A Circle of Quiet

STEWARDSHIP

There's no such thing as a supermom. We just do the best we can.

—*Sarah Michelle Gellar, American actress and philanthropist*

STRENGTH

DAY 342

A mother is the truest friend we have, when trials heavy and sudden fall upon us; when adversity takes the place of prosperity; when friends desert us; when trouble thickens around us, still will she cling to us and endeavor by her kind precepts and counsels to dissipate the clouds of darkness, and cause peace to return to our hearts.

—*Washington Irving, American author and essayist*

DAY 343

Difficult times have helped me to
understand better than before, how
infinitely rich and beautiful life is in
every way, and that so many things
that one goes worrying about are of
no importance whatsoever.

—*Isak Dinesen, Danish author*

It has long been an axiom of mine that the little things are infinitely the most important.

—Arthur Conan Doyle,
British writer and physician

WISDOM

The best place to cry is on
a mother's arms.

—*Jodi Picoult, American author*

LOVE

The best way to make children
good is to make them happy.

—*Oscar Wilde, Irish author, playwright,
and poet*

HAPPINESS

We cannot always build the future for our youth, but we can build our youth for the future.

—*Franklin D. Roosevelt, former president of the United States*

STEWARDSHIP

DAY 348

All of us have moments in our lives that test our courage. Taking children into a house with a white carpet is one of them.

—Erma Bombeck, American humorist and columnist

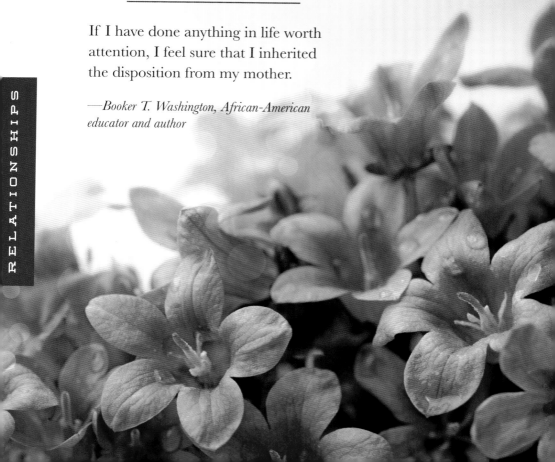

DAY 349

If I have done anything in life worth
attention, I feel sure that I inherited
the disposition from my mother.

—*Booker T. Washington, African-American*
educator and author

BEAUTY

The most beautiful thing we can experience is the mysterious. It is the source of all true art and science.

—*Albert Einstein, German-born theoretical physicist*

WISDOM

Children are people, and they should have to reach to learn about things, to understand things, just as adults have to reach if they want to grow in mental stature. Life is composed of lights and shadows, and we would be untruthful, insincere, and saccharine if we tried to pretend there were no shadows. Most things are good, and they are the strongest things; but there are evil things too, and you are not doing a child a favor by trying to shield him from reality. The important thing is to teach a child that good can always triumph over evil.

—*Walt Disney, American entrepreneur, cartoonist, animator, voice actor, and film producer*

DAY 352

Youth fades; love droops; the leaves of friendship
fall; a mother's secret hope outlives them all.

—*Oliver Wendell Holmes, American physician, poet, and author*

HAPPINESS

DAY 353

People always accuse me of being motivational in a way, like it was a bad thing, but that's just how I was raised. My mom raised me in a positive environment, with lots of love in my heart.

—*Lenny Kravitz, American singer-songwriter*

We all know that parents do not make children but that children make parents. . . . Authentic parenting is one long sacrificial act. . . . Parenting reveals the way that sacrifice at once diminishes our life as we knew it while at the same time revealing to us larger and infinitely more fascinating forms of life. . . . Parents know experientially that the very process which makes them suffer also makes them grow.

—*Luke Timothy Johnson, American Christian scholar and historian,* The Living Gospel

DAY 355

Motherhood is the most completely humbling experience I've ever had.

—*Diane Keaton, American actress*

DAY 356

My mom is my hero. She inspired
me to dream when I was a kid, so
anytime anyone inspires you to
dream, that's gotta be your hero.

—*Tim McGraw, American country music
artist*

The highest and most beautiful things in life are not to be heard about, nor read about, nor seen but, if one will, are to be lived.

—*Soren Kierkegaard, Danish philosopher, theologian, poet, social critic, and religious author*

BEAUTY

DAY 358

Most mothers are instinctive philosophers.

—*Harriet Beecher Stowe, American abolitionist and author*

A flower cannot blossom without sunshine, and man cannot live without love.

—*Friedrich Max Müller, German-born philologist*

LOVE

[Motherhood is] heart-exploding, blissful hysteria.

—*Olivia Wilde, American actress*

HAPPINESS

DAY 361

If you are a parent, open doors to unknown directions to the child so he can explore. Don't make him afraid of the unknown; give him support.

—*Osho, Indian mystic, guru and spiritual teacher*

Endurance is not just the ability to bear a hard thing, but to turn it into glory.

—*William Barclay, Scottish author, radio and television presenter, and minister*

STRENGTH

Be the mom you want them to remember.

—*Unknown*

RELATIONSHIPS

ABOUT FAMILIUS

Welcome to a place where mothers and fathers are celebrated, not belittled. Where values are at the core of happy family life. Where boo-boos are still kissed, cake beaters are still licked, and mistakes are still okay. Welcome to a place where books—and family—are beautiful. Familius: a book publisher dedicated to helping families be happy.

If you feel a few friends and family might benefit from what you've read, let us know and we'll be happy to provide you with quantity discounts. Simply email us at specialorders@familius.com.

Website: www.familius.com
Facebook: www.facebook.com/paterfamilius
Twitter: @familiustalk, @paterfamilius1
Pinterest: www.pinterest.com/familius

The most important work you ever do will be within the walls of your own home.

FAMILIUS

Published by Familius LLC, www.familius.com
1254 Commerce Way, Sanger, CA 93657

Familius books are available at special discounts for bulk purchases, whether for
sales promotions or for family or corporate use. For more information, contact
Familius Sales at 559-876-2170 or email orders@familius.com.

Library of Congress Control Number: 2019952363
ISBN 9781641702249

Compiled and edited by Kelsey Cummings
Book design by David Miles
Cover and jacket design by Carlos Guerrero
Photography credit: Shutterstock.com

10 9 8 7 6 5 4 3 2 1
First Edition
Printed in China